TENERIFE

THE ENGLISH EDITION

© OTERMIN EDICIONES, S. C.
Telf.:   952 29 56 42
Fax.:   952 20 70 36
Dep. Legal: MA-707-2006
ISBN: 84-88187-26-2

Distribución
GARCÍA Y CORREA, S. L.
Santa Cruz de Tenerife
Telf: 922 22 98 40

Santa Cruz de Tenerife

TENERIFE

Tenerife is the largest of the seven isles which make up the Canary Islands. Located between Gran Canaria island (S.E.), and La Gomera (S.W.), its surface area is 2,057 km² and its shape is similar to an isosceles triangle, with its base in the southwest and vertexes in la Punta de Anaga, la Punta de Rasca and la Punta de Teno. It is also the highest island - the Teide rises to 3,718m and is Tenerife's symbol as well as being the highest peak, not only of the islands, but also of the whole of the Spanish territory. Plinio, a naturalist from the first century A.D., relates in his texts how one of the Fortunate Isles stood out due to its perpetual snows, called **«Nivaria»** (snowy island) by the sailors owing to the Teide's white colour.

Portrayed in numerous legendary tales as the remains of a mythical sunken continent, Atlantis, scientific theories consider the islands to be part of a large volcanic chain, located in the contact zone between the oceanic and continental crusts of the African plate, which, during the Alpine orogenia, went through an intense fracturing process resulting in the emergence of a serie of blocks from the oceanic crust and eventually, after intense, submarine volcanic activity, the formation of island blocks.

The island's substratum is almost exclusively eruptive. This volcanic origin greatly detemined its geological characteristics, not only the composition of the rocks and minerals, but also its main geomorphogical landmarks (volcanoes «malpaíses»), all combined in close relationship with the continuous changes produced by erosion through millions of years.

Tenerife's climate is mild, with few seasonal contrasts. Temperatures are moderate, with variations due mainly to altitude. The most characteristic climatic feature is, perhaps, the predominance of anticyclonic conditions, with scarce precipitatation, especially in the south. On the other hand, trade winds bring humidity and uniform temperatures.

Tenerife was present in the mythology of Phoenician, Greek, Carthaginian and Roman sailors. Later, Portuguese, Mallorcan and Genoese sailors began to appear on the coasts and it was in the fifteenth century that the conquest of the archipelago began, with Tenerife the last island to be absorbed by the Castilian crown in 1496. After the discovery of America, Tenerife gained commercial importance at the intersection of sea routes between overseas colonies and the metropolis.

Today, Tenerife is a natural paradise for travellers, with its blend of natural beauty spots and the numerous attractions and contrasts it offers.

Santa Cruz de Tenerife

Panoramic view of Santa Cruz de Tenerife

Santa Cruz de Tenerife, the modern provincial capital, was founded in 1494 in the form of a small fishing village alongside the Añazo beaches (today Puerto de Santa Cruz). It was the nineteenth century which saw it gain a commercial and political presence within the archipelago. Open to the sea, it lies at the foot of the Anaga massif, whose lower slopes play host to **Las Teresitas beach** with its original black sand and its yellow, Saharan sand where palm trees grow. Further along the coast, Las Gaviotas beach and Chica beach, small bays of black sand on the way to Igueste de San Andrés, a leafy valley with a multitude of tropical plant species. A welcoming city, Santa Cruz offers strolls through gardens and along avenues, across attractive, wide squares and down boulevards. The «ramblas» a succession of tree-lined streets, is an original, open-air gallery, to the left of which we find the **García Sanabria park,** a route of exhuberant and varied flora, dominated by the peculiar monument to an ex-mayor and decorated with fountains and tiny squares.

From the higt part of the park, along the 25 de julio «rambla», we reach **Weyler Square,** the gardens of which decorate the outside of the plain Capitanía palace. Another splendid example of civil architecture is the Guimerá theatre, very near to the popular Recoveco de Santa Cruz. In the bustling, commercial centre, next to Candelaria Square and in the grounds of the old San Cristóbal Fortress, is the **Plaza de España** (Spain Square), a magnificent scene of light and colour during the Carnival, and splendid stage for the traditional Winter Festival.

García Sanabria Park. Santa Cruz de Tenerife

García Sanabria Park

Las Teresitas Beach. Santa Cruz de Tenerife

Weyler Square

Guimerá Theatre

Las Teresitas Beach

Plaza de España. Santa Cruz de Tenerife

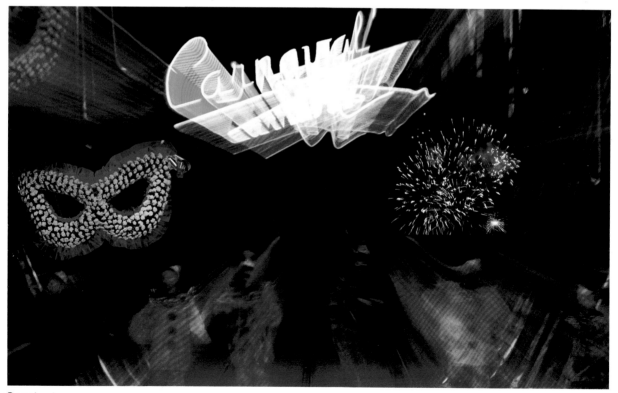

Carnival

Tenerife Auditorium

Parque Marítimo César Manrique. Tenerife Auditorium

Parque Marítimo

Church of La Concepción

Plaza de España

Anaga Massif. Taganana

The **Anaga** massif, which limits and stands guard over Santa Cruz, covers an area of 200 km² in the northeastern part of the island. A peculiar, very eroded, volcanic zone, it is the natural habitat of numerous endemic species, making this a biologically-rich area.

This massif, along with the Teno, Tenerife's ancient massifs, boasts a topography of deep narrow valleys separated by sharp interfluvials which connect with the bottom of the ravines down very steep slopes which, in some cases, form authentic escarpments. It does not reach great heights, with its dominant point being the Cruz de Taborno, at 1,020 m.

On the southern slopes of the massif lie Iguesta, San Andrés, the Teresitas beach and all the Capital's urban and port areas.

On the northern slopes, between mountains, lies the picturesque little town of **Taganana,** whose name goes back to the ancient Guanche settlers. It boasts examples of old-style Canarian dwellings and crowns the steep northern zone just before the land descends into the clean coastal waters.

View of La Laguna from the Monte de las Mercedes

La Laguna

Monte de las Mercedes

From Las Mercedes mountain we can enjoy a panorama of **San Cristobal de La Laguna,** the capital of the La Laguna district, a name which recalls the old geographical configuration of this area, which is still part of the Anaga region and is only nine kilometres from Santa Cruz.

An episcopal, cathedral and university city, its streets still hold memories of the old colonial design. Its monumental, historical centre, a showroom of real jewels of civil and religious architecture, houses, amongst others, the **Cathedral,** where the image of the Crucified Christ (Cristo crucificado de los Remedios) can be worshipped as it stands on its majectic tabernacle.

La Laguna Cathedral, officially opened in 1913, combines the Neogothic style - unmistakable on the inside and in the presbytery with its four marble altar steps - with the neoclassical style of the main doorway, as a result of the reconstruction following the decision that the original Nuestra Señora de los Remedios Church was in a ruinous state. It became a Cathedral in 1818 when the diocese of Tenerife was created.

Due to a strong cultural tradition and thanks to the initiative of the Augustinian order, founded at the beginning of the sixteenth century, in 1744 Santa Cruz obtained the rank of university city. The old Saint Ferdinard University, built in 1817, has a wide façade and luxurious forms.

Inside the cathedral. La Laguna

Cristo de los Remedios. La Laguna Cathedral

La Laguna University

Nowadays, it is possible to study almost all existing university courses in this centre.

La Laguna is an agricultural town which spreads north along the Guerra, Tegueste and Tejina valley to the coastal zone around **Bajamar** and **Punta del Hidalgo,** a calm, touristic town, surprising due to the number of natural bays to be discovered along its coast.

Tacoronte is wine territory. A region marked by deep gullies, it nevertheless offers hillsides and valleys overflowing with vineyards over an area of almost 2,500 hectars, the largest and densest vineyards in the Canary Islands.

It enjoyed great prestige at the end of the sixteenth century, with its malmsey wine praised throughout Europe and in the newly colonised American markets. The decline set in at the end of seventeenth century in favour of Portuguese wines, greatly helped by the mildew and plague in the second half of the nineteenth century.

From then on, relegated to the ranks of a family and craft industry, Tacaronte today symbolises the return of Canarian wine. Produced in the varieties «listán» and «negramoll», mild, full and aromatic, Tacaronte's red wine is a magnificent table wine. Fresh and with a special aroma, it is the inseparable companion of the rich and varied Canarian food.

Punta del Hidalgo

Punta del Hidalgo

Tacoronte. Bodegas Alvaro

Tufuriaste House. Pottery museum in La Orotava

Flora in Anaga Massif

Tomatoes

Typical cooking

Country women in Punta de Anaga

Tufuriaste House museum. La Orotava

La Orotava is another of Tenerife's natural regions and corresponds almost exactly with the rich Taoro «menceyato», one of the kingdoms created by the ancient Guanche settlers when they divided the island. It is dominated by the valley of the same name and is an area rich in water and dependent on the intense banana cultivation.

In the valley's coastal zone, at the bottom of a gentle slope which begins in the Teide's nearby volcanic massif, lies the Canary Islands' smallest town, which is, nevertheless, one of the world's most important tourist resorts: **El Puerto de la Cruz.**

The Lake Martiánez installations are an internationally-recognised emblem of our modern times, work of the famous artist **César Manrique,** where water and vegetation merge with the landscape in surroundings which are extraordinary for the original quality of the architecture.

A walk through the port offers the chance to visit both the bustling, crowded tourist centre and peaceful squares with gardens where one can have a quiet conversation in the shade of a laurel or a Canarian palm. Quintana street, which leads to Nuestra Señora de la Peña de Francia Square or to Charco Square and San Felipe Street, are examples of the cosmopolitan environment, where the genuine character of the people may be perceived.

Puerto de La Cruz

Puerto de La Cruz

Puerto de La Cruz →

Martiánez Lake. Puerto de la Cruz

Detail

Puerto de la Cruz from Martiánez Lake

View of Lake Martiánez

Swimming-pool. Martiánez Lake

Puerto de La Cruz

Loro Park. Puerto de La Cruz. Flamencos

Orquid Garden

Loro Park. Details

Balearica pavonina

Acuarium in Loro Park

Tourism is undoubtedly one of the more important sources of income for the island and noticeably stimulates other sectors such a transport and construction. Tenerife's warm climate and natural beauty hold a powerful attraction for Spaniards as well as for foreigners. The number of visitors increases year by year and has now passed two million. This inevitably affects the character and lifestyle of the Canarian population and their need to assert their personality and maintain their idiosyncrasy and identity.

In Puerto de la Cruz there are two essential touristic visits to be made: one, on the Icod Road, next to the Punta Brava district, is **Loro Parque** (Parrot Park). An area of more than 50,000 m² houses more than 300 species of parrot in a collection considered to be the best in the world. There is also a dolphin park, a magnificent orchid garden where a wide variety of beautiful, delicate flowers may be admired and facilities for other species of animals and plants.

The second is the **Jardín Botánico** (Botanical Gardens) - reached by the road of the same name - which was created in 1788, during Carlos III's reign, by Alonso de Nava Grimón, sixth Marquis of Villanueva del Prado. His aim was to acclimatize plant species from America, Africa and Asia, once the gardens of Aranjuez and Madrid had been ruled out due to the harsh winter temperatures. Its centennial history has its origins in the free concession of land by Francisco de Lugo y Saavedra, Lord of Fuerteventura Island, the donation of the necessary water by the Orotava Gentlemen's Water Board and the design of the original plans by an architect from La Laguna, who also worked on Las Palmas cathedral. From that moment

Loro Parque . Puerto de La Cruz

Punta Brava beach. Puerto de La Cruz

onwards it suffered numerous transformations due to its high maintenance costs, which at times brought into question its very existence, such as in 1850 when the island Governor put it up for rent, to be saved only thanks to the private efforts of José Bethancourt de Castro. There followed changes to the original design, dependence on different institutions such as the Royal Economic Society of Friends of the Country (*Real Sociedad Económica de Amigos del País*), the official Agricultural Chamber of La Orotava, (*Cámara Oficial de Agricultura de La Orotava*), from 1906 and the National Institute for Agricultural Research (*Instituto Nacional de Investigaciones Agronómicas*), from 1941. Praise was never lacking from noteworthy travellers and scientist's such as Baudin, Humboldt or Masferrer. The arrival on the island of the Swiss botanist Enrique S. Sventenius was vital for the development of the garden, as the work of

Botanical Gardens. Puerto de la Cruz (Coussaboa de   Albata)

Botanical Gardens

Hermann Wildpredt or the Catalonian, Juan Bolinaga, had been before him. Sventenius began to organize the herb gardens and to study in detail the Canarian Flora. In 1944 the first guide of the gardens was published along with the Index Seminum for national and international exchanges. SInce 1983 the garden has answered to the Autonomous Community and has been linked to the Centre for Agricultural Research and Technology (Centro de Investigación y Tecnología Agrarias), which is part of the Agriculture and Fishing Council (Consejería de Agricultura y Pesca).

Nowadays, the Orotova Plant Acclimatization Garden (Jardín de Aclimatización de Plantas de La Orotova), which is its full name, holds a complete collection of species from all over the world and is the Canarian Community's contribution to international research and teaching, as well as a beautiful place to learn and relax for its many visitors.

La Orotava

Alejandro de Humboldt, a geographer and naturalist; visited the island in 1799 and communicated to the entire world his vision of the Orotava valley's incomparable beauty. Today, from the viewpoint which carries his name, we may contemplate a beautiful panoramic view of all the valley, sown with banana groves, in which lies one of the oldest towns of the island: **La Orotava.** Here stands the most important example in the Canary Islands of the Barroque style: **la Iglesia de la Concepción.** This is a national monument, built in the second half of the eighteenth century. It has a magnificent barroque façade with rococo elements and inside boasts sculptures, paintings and bas-reliefs in its altarpiece. The city is famous for the colourful carpets of volcanic sands which decorate the Plaza del Ayuntamiento each year in the Corpus Christi celebrations and as centre of excellent Canarian craftsmanship in linen weave and wood. The wooden artwork may be appreciated in the special designs of the balconies which adorn many of the houses in La Orotava, dating back to the seventeenth and eighteenth centuries and reflecting its aristocratic tradition.

Next to the Orotava valley, between the Tigaiga and Teno massifs, lies the region of Icod, the old Guanche name which became **Icod de los Vinos** thanks to the successful cultivation of grapes. In this town is to be found the emblematic symbol of the Canarian Flora: **the Dragon tree** (el Drago), which tradition considers to be millennial. This species was an importance resource for the ancient Guanche population: they ate its fruit, built houses and weapons with its wood and made medicines from its red sap.

Further to the west, by the sea, lying on a lava plain, is **Garachico,** a name which combines the ancient Guanche root «igara» - island - with the Spanish adjective «chico» - small-, in reference to the rock which can be seen just off the coast.

Los Balcones House. La Orotava

La Concepción church. La Orotava.

Icod de Los Vinos. Millennial Dragon Tree

1000 year-old Dragon Tree

Icod de Los Vinos

La Orotava Valley

Church of San Marcos. Icod de Los Vinos

1000 year-old Dragon Tree

La Orotava Valley

Banana Plantations

Garachico →

La Caleta from Tanque

Buenavista del Norte

Punta Morro del Diablo from Don Pompeyo viewpoint

Don Pompeyo viewpoint. Buenavista del Norte

Garachico shares the northern slopes of the Teno region with the towns **El Tanque, Los Silos** and **Buenavista,** at the western end of Tenerife. It is a region of contrasts between the shallow valleys of the north, which form the so-called Low Island (Isla Baja) and the imposing cliffs of the southern slopes. In El Tanque traditional buildings and crops are still conserved in a rugged area without a coastline, witness to the eruption of the Montaña Negra or Trevejo Volcano in 1706.

Buenavista del Norte has a landscape which is characteristic of this region: one almost flat zone, another with high plateaux and another large zone formed by the plains of the Teno massif's natural park. This variety forms an extraordinarily attractive landscape in a succession of scattered, distant districts which spread as far as the **Punta de Teno**. Here stands the old Teno lighthouse **(Faro de Teno)**, which is out of use nowadays but which began to work at the end of the nineteenth century. The town of Buenavista del Norte was founded in 1513, a detail conserved thanks to the city's founding document, which in kept in the the Town Hall, a building in the Neocanarian style, like others on the island. In the church, the patron saint of the town, Nuestra Señora de los Remedios, has three gold locusts embroidered on her robe in remembrance of the miracle attributed to the virgin when she rid the population of a plague of locusts in 1659.

Punta de Teno

Teno lighthouse

Papayas at Punta Negra

An especially attractive tourist offering is a little hamlet named **Masca**. Here we may observe an exquisite example of typical Canarian primitive rural architecture. Maca's impressive gully extends down onto a black sand beach surrounded on bolt sides by high cliffs.

Gullies are deep, narrow gashes in the earth which, from their highest point down to the sea, act as a channel for possible torrential waters. The special characteristics of the island's relief, with a large number of gullies formed by volcanic activity, explains the fact that, unlike many civilizations who settled near to rivers and valleys, in Tenerife the Guanche people settled close to gullies. Many of the present day settlements were established in this way. The gullies often prevent towns from extending further.

The coastline has numerous, high, steep cliffs, especially in the North and the West of the island, due to the Teide's central, dominating position and its steep slopes which extend all

Teno Massif. Masca

Masca gulley

Arriba Valley. Santiago del Teide   La Arena beach →

the way down to the sea. On the southern side of the Teno massif are the most surprising cliffs in Tenerife, **Los Gigantes** (the Giants), which are as high as 500m at some points.

Moving south from Teno, Santiago de Teide lies in a valley, very near to the hamlet of Arguayo and the volcano Chinyero, which covered the area with lava in 1909, the most recent volcanic eruption in Tenerife. **Arguayo** is also know for its pottery, with its reproductions of the original shapes and decorations peculiar to the ancient inhabitants of the valley.

Guía de Isoro, also in the natural region of Isora, which occupies all the southeastern edge of the island, from the Teno massif to Infierno Gulley, is a living example of the persistence of a farming population who have turned stony, lava territory - «el malpaís» (the bad country) - into a fertile area of almond trees and the most important tomato crop on the island. The town's patron saint, the Virgen de la Cruz de Guía (the Guiding Light Virgin), halted the water which threatened to lay waste to the land after the Chinyero eruption. In thanks for this the locals still hold a yearly celebration in the month of May, the traditional pilgrimage to the dreaded volcano.

In **Santiago del Teide** stands Saint Fernando Rey church, a small, seventeenth century building where the Christ of the Valley's image is revered. Its construction was ordered by Fernando del Hoyo, Lord of the Valley of Santiago, the feudal governer of the region. On its coast, Santiago del Teide has a pretty, warm bay, the **Playa de la Arena** (Sandy Beach) and the picturesque fishing district, Puerto Santiago.

Los Gigantes cliff

Highest quality hotel infrastructure, Costa Adeje

The deep gullies and proud cliffs give way to gentle beaches and dunes in the southwest of the island, hosts to important tourist resorts. The most important of all, the **Playa de las Américas** (Americas' beach), belongs partly to the town of Adeje, where according to legend the great Tinerfe resided, a Guanche lord who governed all Tenerife and partly to the town o Arona, in permanent growth since becoming a tourist resort. Very nearby and practically joined to Playa de las Américas is **Los Cristianos,** a communication point with the other islands which conserves its character as a port and fishing centre, as well as being a popular tourist resort thanks to its wide, golden beach. Finally, on the **Costa del Silencio** lies the district **Las Galletas** with a beach of the same name and a popular meeting point for diving enthusiasts.

Still in the natural region of Chasna, the Guanche name for the entire southern side, the town of **Granadilla** stands near the second highest peak of the island, the Pico Guajara. Moving down towards the coast, we cross a zone of eroded, volcanic cones and material from the two recent eruptions of the eighteenth century, until we reach the longest beaches of the island: La Tejita and **El Médano beach** is a zone of strong, constant winds and the ideal place for windsurfing, a sport which boosts the local tourist industry with its international competitions.

Beach at Duque Costa Adeje

Beach at Duque, Seafront promenade at Costa Adeje

Costa Adeje

Costa Adeje

Golf course

Playa de Las Américas

Los Cristianos

Los Cristianos. Marina

Las Galletas beach

Hondo Gulley

Legend has it that, before conquering the island, Guanches found a Gothic carving which they placed in a cave and worshipped, giving it the name Chaxiraxi o Señora del Mundo (Lady of the World). From then on this city's history has been linked to the **Virgen de la Candelaria,** proclaimed patron saint of the Canary Islands in 1599 by Pope Clement VIII. The modern-day image of the Virgin - the original, primitive one was lost in a flood in 1826 - is worshipped in la Capilla Mayor de la Basílica, a place of pilgrimage for Canarians each August 15 when they celebrate the Virgin's Festival. Opposite the Basilica and guarded by statues of Guanche lords is the black sand beach which, along with Las Caletillas beach, represents the regional hopes to become part of the tourist development taking place in other zones of the island. Candelaria still conserves houses in the tradition Canarian style in a number of its districts.

Flor de Pascua. (Euphorbia pulcherrima)

Banana grove

Paradise bird. (Strelitzia reginae)

Médano beach ➜

Hibiscus rosa-sinensis

Tajinaste

Médano beach

Candelaria.

Candelaria

Nuestra Señora de la Candelaria basilica

Virgen de la Candelaria

La Candelaria beach

Etymologically speaking, the word **«Guanche»** means «man from Tenerife». Tall, robust, strong men, according to ancient tales they were mainly animal farmers, although they still had time to grow wheat and barley and to fish. They dressed in animal skins and had a basic diet of meat and milk, which they complemented with ground, toasted grain (gofio), fish, fruit and honey. They lived in caves organized around a central fire, flanked by an entrance wall and decorated with stone furniture covered with skins or dried grasses and lit by clay lamps fueled with animal fat. They wore skins sown using goat guts and goat bone punches and their jewellery consisted of clay bead necklaces or seashells and small stones. They buried their dead and practised embalming as a sign of social position. They believed in one God, who they invoked from the mountain tops, although they admitted the existence of other powers and of Good and Evil spirits. They educated their children with physical and athletic exercises and taught them to detest certain types of behaviour. They divided Tenerife into nine kingdoms or «meceyatos», governed by **Mencey**, advised by his counsellors on social and political questions in a square formed by a circle of stones, called «tagoror». Here he also dealt out punishments according to laws which condemned theft, murder and lack of respect for women, but which did not include the death penalty. They held festivals, for the coronation of a new king and the tradition Beñesmén at the beginning of summer, in which they danced, sang and competed in tests of skill and strength. They demonstrated their stamina and strength in a wrestling match, using wooden clubs, which came to an end when the competitor proved his superiority over his opponent.

On the other side of the mountain from the Orotava valley lies the **Güímar Valley,** a rich agricultural zone which benefits from an abundant water supply from numerous springs and

Güímar

Wind Park

Pottery Centre at Arguayo

Ethnological Museum, Arguayo

underground galleries, favouring the cultivation of vines and cereals in the region's inland zones and banana or avocado pears on the coast.

The origin of the Güímar Valley is not exactly volcanic. It is a valley between hills along the line of a vein of less intense eruptive activity, sandwiched between sectors of greater volcanic activity, which gave rise to mountainous formations and left a structural vacuum in between.

In **Güímar**, the name of an ancient Guanche kingdom, district capital and the most important town in the valley, the natural beauty spot known as Malpaís de Güímar is worthy of a visit. It is an area in which numerous endemic Canarian species are still conserved.

Very near to Güímar is **Arafo**, with origins in the timber industry and known for its wines. It holds prizes for its beauty as a traditional Canarial hamlet and has a deeply-rooted musical tradition.

Panoramic view towards the Cumbres viewpoint

View of the Teide from the Ortuño viewpoint

THE TEIDE NATIONAL PARK

Tenerife, along with the rest of the islands in the archipelago, forms part of the so-called Macaronesic region, which also includes the islands Cabo Verde, Azores, Medeira and Savage. This region is distinguished by its mixture of Mediterranean and Atlantic elements as well as others of a tropical nature. The whole area is considered as authentic international heritage due to the fact that it houses a wide range of endemic plant and animal species which disappeared from the rest of Europe during the ice ages.

In the Canary Islands a third of the vascular plants are endemic species. In addition to the Teide National Park, Tenerife has 22 protected natural areas and 6 natural parks.

The **Parque Nacional del Teide** (Teide National Park) or the **Cañadas del Teide** (Teides's Gullies) was declared a National Park in 1954 and at the present spreads over 13,571 hectars, which may be extended in the future.

It includes the Cañadas zone in which the majestic **Teide Volcano** rises to **3,718** metres above sea level.

Las Cañadas is an enormous crater with a diameter of some 16 km., surrounded by a semicircular mountain chain formed by lava defiles and intercalated with basalt. Entry is by

Teide National Park

Teide National Park

Teide National Park

way of two natural doors: on the northern side the Portillo de las Cañadas or Portillo de la Villa (2,000 m.) and on the southwestern side the Boca de Tauce (2,100 m.).

The Teide National Park contains an astonishing variety of plant life, with some 139 superior species, 30 of wich endemic, to be found only in the park. This flora is surprising due to being perfectly adapted to altitude, sun, low night-time temperatures and drought.

The most common typical plant in the park is the Teide Broom (Spartocytisus supranubius), wich is to be found almost everywhere and helps shape the park's landscape. Another spectacular plant, rightly nicknamed «pride of Tenerife», is the Red «Tajinaste» (Echium wildpretii), wich grows on the eroded sides of the Crater to a height of almost 3 metres, with its typical inflorescences in clusters of intense red flowers. The Teide Daisy is a species to be found only in the park, different from all the other daisies in the world with its long, regular, white and yellow petals. The park's flora is enriched by numerous endemic, Macaronesic species. Worthy of a special mention are the blue-flowered Teide Grass (Nepeta teydea) and the Teide Wallflower (Erysimun scoparium), with flowers of a pink-lilac colour. Two authentic plant treasures are the Guanche Rose (Bencomia stipulata) and the Teide Violet (Viola cheiranthifolia), wich grows on the sides of the volcanic cone.

Los Roques

Roque Cinchado in the Teide National Park

The park also offers the possibility to make excursions along various routes, a real brush with nature with unexpected surprises at every step.

The mirador de la Ruleta is an essential stop, in the centre of the large Cañadas craters. On one side stand the admirable **Roques de García**, the skeleton of a wall which separated two semicraters and on the other side the **Ucanca Valley**, the widest crater in the park.

Worthy of mention is the **Roque Cinchado**, a rock in the shape of a tree, more than 20 m. high, familiar to everybody because it appears on the back of the one thousand pesetas notes.

Outside the park, in the Izaña area, near to the Portillo de las Cañadas, stands the **Teide Astrophysics Observatory,** at a height of 2,392 m., in which several European countries have installed telescopes in order to study solar physics. It is considered to be one of the most important observatories in the world.

Izaña Astrophysics Observatory

San José Mines

Teide National Park

LLano de Ucanca

LLano de Ucanca

Teide National Park

Sunset in the teide National Park

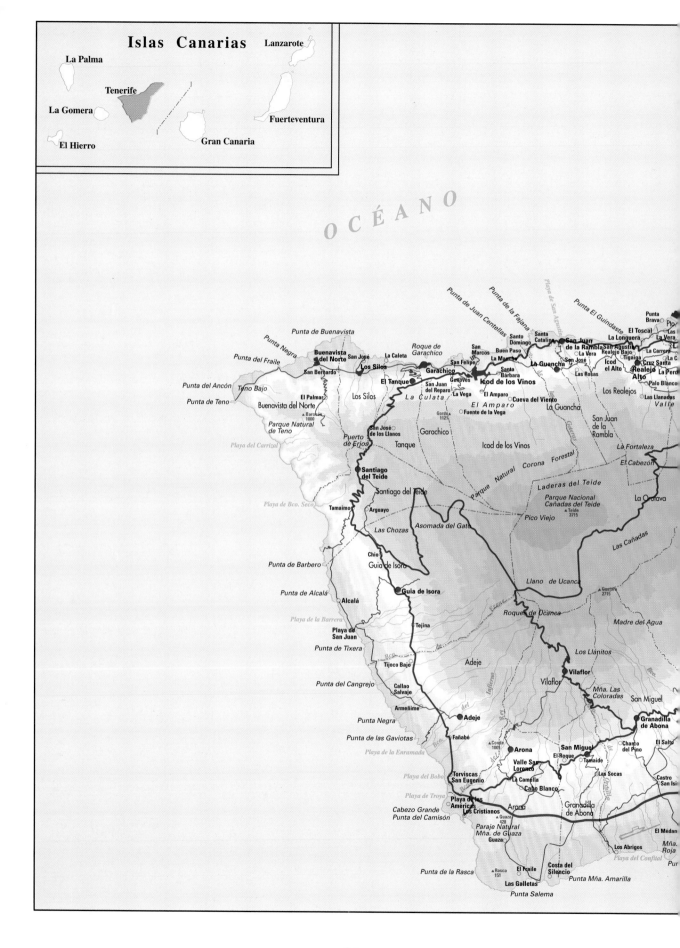

Islas Canarias

La Palma

Lanzarote

Tenerife

La Gomera

Fuerteventura

El Hierro

Gran Canaria

OCÉANO

Punta de Buenavista

Punta Negra

Punta del Fraile

Roque de Garachico

Punta de Juan Centellas

Punta de la Fajana

Punta El Guindaste

Punta Brava

Pto.

Santo Domingo

Santa Catalina

San Juan de la Rambla

El Toscal

Las

La Vera

La Longuera

San Agustín

Buenavista del Norte

San José

La Caleta

San Marcos

San Felipe

Buen Paso

La Guancha

La Vera

Realejo Bajo

La C

La Carrera

San Bernardo

Los Silos

Garachico

La Mancha

Santa Bárbara

Sen José

Icod el Alto

Tigaiga

Cruz Santa

La Perd

Punta del Ancón

El Tanque

San Juan del Reparo

La Vega

Icod de los Vinos

El Amparo

Las Rosas

Realejo Alto

Palo Blanco

Punta de Teno

Teno Bajo

Los Silos

La Culata

Cueva del Viento

Los Realejos

Las Llanadas

Valle

El Palmar

Gordo 1000

El Amparo

La Guancha

Punta del Fraile

Buenavista del Norte

Gordo 1121

Fuente de la Vega

San Juan de la Rambla

Parque Natural de Teno

San José de los Llanos

Garachico

Là Fortaleza

Playa del Carrizal

Puerto de Erjos

Tanque

Icod de los Vinos

El Cabezón

Santiago del Teide

Parque Natural Corona Forestal

Laderas del Teide

Playa de Bco. Seco.

Santiago del Teide

La Orotava

Tamaimo

Arguayo

Parque Nacional Cañadas del Teide

▲ Teide 3715

Las Chozas

Asomada del Gato

Pico Viejo

Las Cañadas

Chio

Guía de Isora

Llano de Ucanca

Punta de Barbero

▲ Guajara 2715

Punta de Alcalá

Alcalá

Guía de Isora

Roques de Ucanca

Madre del Agua

Playa de la Barrera

Tejina

Los Llanitos

Playa de San Juan

Punta de Tixera

Adeje

Vilaflor

Tijoco Bajo

Vilaflor

Mña. Las Coloradas

San Miguel

Punta del Cangrejo

Callao Salvaje

Armeñime

Adeje

Granadilla de Abona

Punta Negra

Fañabé

▲ Conde 1001

San Miguel

Charco del Pino

El Salto

Punta de las Gaviotas

Arona

El Roque

Tamaide

Playa de la Enramada

Valle San Lorenzo

Las Socas

Torviscas San Eugenio

La Camélla

Castro San Isi

Playa del Bobo

Cabo Blanco

Granadilla de Abona

Playa de Troya

Playa de las Américas

Arona

Cabezo Grande Punta del Camisón

Los Cristianos

▲ Guaza 428

El Médan

Paraje Natural Mña. de Guaza

Guaza

Mña. Roja

Los Abrigos

Playa del Confital

Pur

Punta de la Rasca

▲ Rasca 151

El Fraile

Costa del Silencio

Las Galletas

Punta Mña. Amarilla

Punta Salema

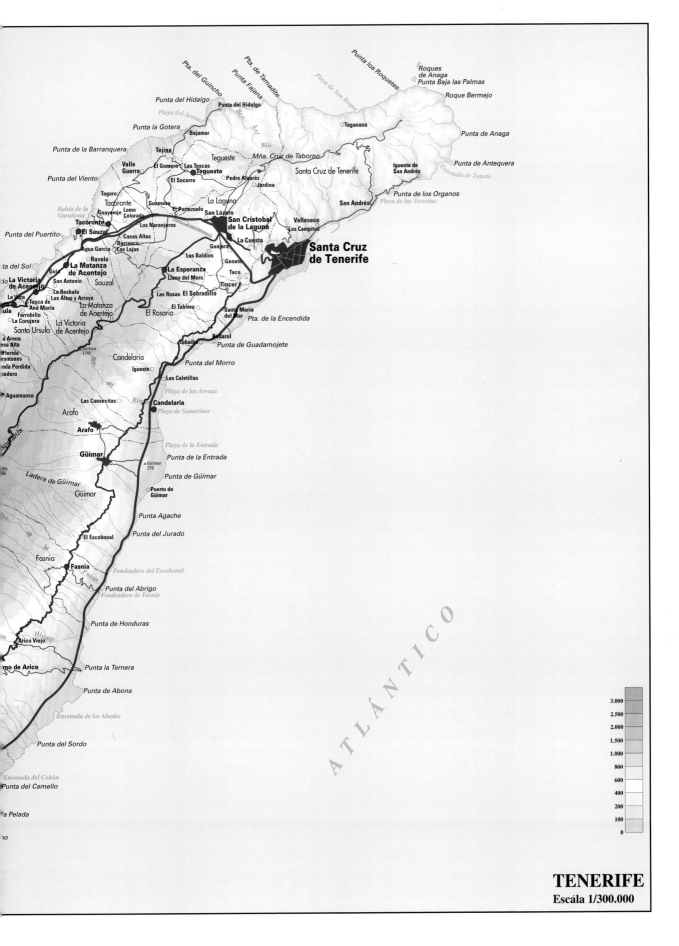

Pta. del Guincho Pta. de Tamadite Punta los Roquetes Roques de Anaga Punta Baja las Palmas
Punta Fajana Roque Bermejo
Punta del Hidalgo **Punta del Hidalgo** Playa de San Roque
Playa del Arenal Taganana Punta de Anaga
Punta la Gotera **Bajamar**
Punta de la Barranquera **Tejina** Tegueste Mña. Cruz de Taborno Santa Cruz de Tenerife Punta de Antequera
Valle Guerra **El Gomero** Las Toscas **Tegueste** Iguesté de San Andrés Ensenada de Zapata
Punta del Viento El Socorro Pedro Álvarez
Tagoro Guamasa Jardina Punta de los Organos
Tacoronte Guayonje El Portezuelo La Laguna San Andrés Playa de las Teresitas
Bahía de la Garañona Lomo Colorado San Lázaro
Tacoronte Los Naranjeros **San Cristobal de la Laguna** Valleseco
El Sauzal Casas Altas **La Cuesta** Los Campitos **Santa Cruz de Tenerife**
Punta del Puertito Barranco Guajara
Agua Garcia Las Lajas Los Baldíos
Ravelo Geneto
ta del Sol **La Matanza de Acentejo** Guia San Antonio **La Esperanza** Taco
La Victoria de Acentejo La Resbala Sauzal Llano del Moro Tinçer
La Vera Los Altos y Arroyo Las Rosas **El Sobradillo**
ula Tosca de Ana María **La Matanza de Acentejo** El Tablero
Farrobillo El Rosario Santa María del Mar Pta. de la Encendida
La Corujera
Santa Ursula La Victoria de Acentejo
Arena Badazul
sa Alta Tabaiba Punta de Guadamojete
Florida Teide Candelaria Punta del Morro
ontones 1745
anda Perdida Igueste
edero Las Caletillas
Playa de las Arenas
Aguamansa Las Cuevecitas **Candelaria**
Arafo Playa de Samarines
Arafo Playa de la Entrada
Güimar Punta de la Entrada
Ladera de Güimar Güimar 276
Güimar Punta de Güimar
Puerto de Güimar
Punta Agache
El Escobonal Punta del Jurado
Fasnia Fondeadero del Escobonal
Fasnia Punta del Abrigo
Fondeadero de Fasnia
Punta de Honduras
Arico Viejo
mo de Arico Punta la Ternera
Punta de Abona
Ensenada de los Abades
Punta del Sordo
Ensenada del Cobón
Punta del Camello
a Pelada
io

A T L Á N T I C O

	3.000
	2.500
	2.000
	1.500
	1.000
	800
	600
	400
	200
	100
	0

TENERIFE
Escala 1/300.000

Portada:

Teide National Park

Contraportada:

Panoramic view. In the background, Santa Cruz de Tenerife